1

"I turn to simplicity;

I turn again to purity."

—Genghis Khan. 1221.

Many years ago, when I had a proper job in an advertising agency, I worked down the corridor from a guy called Neil French.

Neil was a bit of an advertising legend. Early in his career, he'd caused chaos at an awards show when the judges realised they'd given most of the gongs not just to a single advertising agency, but to a single *person* in that agency.

Anyway, one fine day—after a bottle of Rioja, or for a bet, or something—Neil wrote a little book. A *very* little book. Just 32 postcard-sized pages.

That little book contained *everything* anyone would ever need to know about the advertising business. It was called "How to do Ads".

Three continents later, that little book is still on my shelf. (A bit bedraggled, obvs.) I saw it again recently. And it got me wondering.

Since I left the employed life, I've learned a lot about the way many people work today: in the gig economy, or "freelance". In fact, I've written a large book on it. A *very* large book*.

But could I write a *little* book on freelancing too, summing up the basic principles of indie success?

48 hours later, it was done. You be the judge.

CHRIS WORTH

* 100days100grand.com. (Sorry. Had to get that in.)

WHAT IS FREELANCING?

Freelancing is about "following your passion" or "doing your own thing", right? **Wrong**.

The wannabe novelist, the garage tinkerer, the artist with a garretful of canvases only liked by his Mum are not "freelancers". Nor is the lissom nymph 'gramming from Bali, or the shredded hunk "crushing it" on YouTube. That's them *not* freelancing. (If you doubt this, count how many make a living at it.)

And there's the clue. Freelancing is the skill *someone pays for*. Which means doing stuff for *other* people.

If nobody's paying you for what you do, it's not your business, it's your hobby.

So tattoo this on your forehead: *freelancing is about*

earning money.

Mercenary? Nope. There's *nothing* wrong with money. Money is *brilliant*. And money from freelancing is the best kind. It's proof that someone, somewhere, believed the value you created with your head and hands was worth paying for. That's why freelancing, done right, is the most satisfying work you'll ever do.

You will **not** be a successful freelancer if you think it's not about the money. (Many, *many* people make this mistake.) So, the first lesson of freelancing: understand there's a difference between what you want to do and what the market will pay for. They'll overlap. But they're not the same thing.

BUSINESS BASICS

More books have been written on business than Mötley Crüe has had groupies. But in the end, they all say the same thing. Here it is—the secret of business:

People buy stuff they like, from people they like.

So all you need to do is find people who like you, and do that thing they like for them. For money, natch.

Sounds ~~rude~~ easy? As you'd guess, it's not. But for a different reason than in times past.

Once, finding people to sell to was the hard part. Buccaneering traders made risky voyages, fought bloody wars, and massacred indigenous peoples in the search for custom. Today—with billions using social media, watching YouTube, connecting on LinkedIn, chatting on WhatsApp—*finding* people is easy. It's *engaging* with them that's the problem.

At first glance it seems there's so many businesses out there, and so many freelancers doing great work for them, that there's nothing left for you. The truth is the opposite. In this superabundant, hyperconnected world, there are more customers for what you do than you could *ever* deal with. Millions, even billions.

And all a successful freelancer needs is a few regulars. (Between 3 and 8, if you want the numbers.)

So that's Lesson Two: there *are* customers out there who'll pay you, *whatever* you do. And the first step towards finding them is to decide **what to sell**.

FINDING YOUR USP

In other words, you need a **Unique Selling Proposition**. An offer to the market that covers what you do and the value your customer will get.

The term USP came in with the dinosaurs. (Or the 60s, which is the same thing.) But don't worry if this week's social media hipster scoffs that it's obsolete. There are only about six basic principles in marketing, and they were all discovered long ago. 99% of today's "marketing gurus" are just selling old ideas with jazzier names.

Why "unique"? Because the successful freelancer must demonstrate what *differentiates* their offer from their competitors.

Some think this limits their market, and go generic. Which results in enough competitors to fill a stadium and makes pricing a race to the bottom. Lesson Three: the more market you try to gather in, the more customers will slip through your fingers.

You do your USP *first*, *before* you fret about finding customers. (Reason: there are customers out there for *anything*, as long as your value-add is clear. Think superabundance.) There are many ways to find a USP, but the best for freelancers involves answering **Four Big Questions**. You'll need some paper and pens: A3 and Sharpies work best. (Keeping this simple stops you overthinking it.)

On one sheet, write the question: **what do you love?** Scribble down *everything* that comes to mind, in big honkin' lists. ==Include the silly stuff.== People, places, paintings; rock ballads, movie moments, favourite books, old pairs of jeans, even that 50p spatula you liked the look of in Tesco. You'll build up a picture of the preferences that define what matters here: **you**.

On another sheet, answer **what are you best at?** List your skills, qualifications, everything you're expert in and certified for. Again, **silly stuff matters**. Yes, include languages, work experience, and that PhD in theoretical physics, but put rubberband-flicking and making paper aeroplanes down too.

(There's a reason for this. There'll also be overlap with your first sheet. That's okay.)

Label a third sheet **what does the market need?** In

what circumstances, no matter when or where, did you think: "Someone should fix that"? Long queues. Customer service failures. Stuff that didn't work. Processes that snapped. Write it down: all the stuff that annoys *you*.

Head your last sheet **what will customers pay for?** Businesses pay for whatever saves money, boosts sales, keep customers happy, and so on. Add the detail. That guy who waters the plants: is that *all* he does? What's different about your fave restaurant? Why do people prefer Audis to Skodas? **Think**. And be *precise*. It's specific cases that illustrate the general.

Now you've got your lists, it's time to make the magic happen. Set them all out, side by side . . . look *across* the pages . . . and look for *ideas that connect somehow*.

You appreciate the engine note of an Audi, you've got a degree in maths, and that videogame soundtrack didn't feel right. Hey, maybe that's an issue *you* could fix. (Gaming is a $100bn business.) Or you love parties, taught cram school, and feel strangely unsatisfied when you visit that noodle chain. Maybe *you're* the guy to pep up their staff training. (A $40bn sector.) Or you studied coding, and get irritated that mortgage applications never ask the right questions? Maybe banks need a process redesigned. ($Trillions.) Make concepts play with each other and see what results. (It's called "Idea Sex".)

To go even deeper, use **Five Whys**. It's simple: ask yourself why, five times in sequence. *Why* do you like Pizza-a-Go-Go? The Triple Pepperoni? Okay, *why* does that topping make your heart soar? *Why* does it remind you of that place in Portland? By the fifth *Why* you'll have learnt something big.

However you do it, look long and hard and deep. Because ==somewhere in the concepts uniting your four lists is your "signature move". That thing you know needs doing, adds value worth paying for, and you can do better than anyone else.==

What's more, *doing it gives you a buzz*. Which means you'll be happy doing it again and again. Getting better at it every time you do so, providing ever greater value and becoming ever more competitive in the market.

This is the clue to your USP. It's the little square in the middle of this diagram, called the **Purposegram**.

Next, write it down as a case, in a single paragraph. A worked example of how an actual customer would benefit from your actions. Be **precise** and **specific**. Actual names, concrete actions, real numbers. (If you came up with multiple examples? Great! Do it two, three, seventeen times. It'll make it even clearer.)

Why so exact? Because you're looking for a case, not a class. It isn't a general thing anyone can do; it's a *specific* thing *you* can do. The more abstractly (sic) you define it, the more opportunities will pass unnoticed.

With your USP, you've got your **offer to the market**: an offer of value that's uniquely yours. *"I achieve outcome X for customer Y by doing Z."*

(For a laugh, guesstimate your *market opportunity*.

Number of companies with that problem you solve, then value per case of solving it, multiplied together. That's the size of your market. It'll be big.)

That USP is the thing you'll be known for. Best of all, being known for that thing doesn't stop you doing *other* things.

In fact, customers who know your USP have a stronger idea of who you are. And that means you'll be their first choice for *other* work in that general area of expertise. They won't bother traversing the hordes of generica if there's a guy they already know whose work they respect.

(People buy from people they like, remember?)

PRICING YOUR SERVICE

With your offer to the market defined, it's time to get it into saleable form. How will you package your offer?

Some freelancers sell their solution as a product. But most deliver it personally, as a *service*. And that's great. Because while products cost serious money and resources to develop and maintain, you can whomp up a service offer for *free*.

Most freelancers bill by-the-day rather than as-they-sleep. In other words, selling their time. This means to make more money, you can:

a) Work more days;

b) Charge more money.

There are only 365 days in a year. So "working more days" has a limit. (And even 200 booked days a year puts you in the busiest 1%.) 150 days a year is a solid estimate of your chargeable time.

Charging more money has a limit too. But it's higher than you think. The easiest way is to set a **day rate**.

Rule of thumb: as a pay-by-the-day freelancer providing a service, you're worth around 15% of the value you add. If that thing you do saves your customer £10,000 every time you do it, charge £1,500.

If that thing takes you two days, set your day rate as £750. If it takes you three days, £500. If it takes six days, find a way of doing it in three.

(You'll hear lots of boasting about "value-based" or

"market-optimised" pricing in freelancer forums. Ignore them and set a plain-vanilla day rate. It makes acquiring customers far easier.)

Always set your day rate high. You can always discount down. But you can never discount up.

150 days a year at £750 is £112,500. Doing what you love and do best, for people who like you.

Not bad for working three days a week.

ON "PERSONAL BRANDING"

Throw a stick at any "networking event" (ugh) and you'll hit someone talking about "personal brands".

Personal brands are *useless*. And anyone saying otherwise *deserves* to get a stick thrown at them.

Apple is a brand. Tesla is a brand. Amazon is a brand. But you? You're a *person*.

Hide that person behind some abstract idea about how others ought to perceive you, and you're scoring an own goal. Why?

Because you'll look as yawningly generic as every other professional services provider. Which will obscure everything that makes you *you*.

People do business with *people*. *Especially* when it comes to one-person businesses, like freelancers.

And since your USP—your offer to the market—is so closely tied up with your personality, dreams, and desires, you need to live as yourself, not a brand.

By all means, present yourself on LinkedIn and Google as the ideal *solution* to your target customer's problem—just don't try to be that and nothing else.

You are a living, breathing, laughing, farting human being. However honed your skills, it's your *personal* qualities that keep customers looking forward to your next visit, not your professional ones.

You've got your offer. Be yourself when selling it.

MARKETING YOURSELF

So you've got your USP. An idea on pricing. And consigned "personal branding" to the rotting pit of hell from whence it came.

Next up is the bit that makes 'em sit up and sing: *winning customers*.

And that means **marketing**. Marketing is the set of activities that introduce potential customers, called *prospects*, to your USP.

After all, no matter how great your offer is, you've still got to tell customers you're there. That means finding the best prospects and converting them into customers at the lowest possible cost.

All great freelancers are great marketers.

Unfortunately, marketing is also the area of business with the highest concentration of complete claptrap. You'll find any number of shady shysters, nonsensical n'er-do-wells, unconvincing consultants whose value is inversely proportional to wackiness of hair, and oddballs with academic pretensions masquerading as the Next Big Thing. Fortunately, you don't have to listen to them.

Your marketing needs just four things. Two documents: a **list** and a **letter**. A tool to manage them, called a **funnel**. And you need a **website**. Sort of.

Here's how to do all four.

YOUR LIST

Many freelancers keep a list of prospective customers. Fewer keep a **List**. The difference between a list and a **List** is *annotation*.

Marketing to a cold list of emails might get 0.1% response, if you're lucky. But a **List** with a few notes personalising each name can drive response rates ten, a hundred times greater.

Why? Name and job title are just *data*. But adding a note on the name's hobbies makes it *information*. Information eats data for lunch. Annotate your List, and you'll know the names on it as *people*.

(People buy from . . . well, if that isn't clear by now it

never will be.)

So your marketing starts with a **List**. You build it in two parts: companies and people.

Your source for finding companies is your four sheets of A3 you scribbled up earlier. (You didn't throw them away, did you?) Your scribblings are marketing gold: they contain all the stuff that interests you. Use them as keywords to search Google for companies interested in the same stuff.

(You'll be surprised how far this can take you. One outdoorsy copywriter found himself a customer that made parts for freeze-dry machinery.)

Finding people is the job of **LinkedIn**, the freelancer's friend. There are a huge number of ways to track down people in companies you like the look of. You can search the company itself, listing employees with a LinkedIn profile. You can sweat your own network, checking if you know a guy who knows a guy. You can lean on your university alumni, seeing if a classmate works there now. Lesson whatever-it-was: use **LinkedIn**.

When you find an interesting sales prospect, look at his or her LinkedIn Profile for a minute. Note down any likes and dislikes, mutual friends, common interests, anything that could forge a bond between you. Put that person and your notes on a spreadsheet. Then do it again. And again. And again.

That's your **List**.

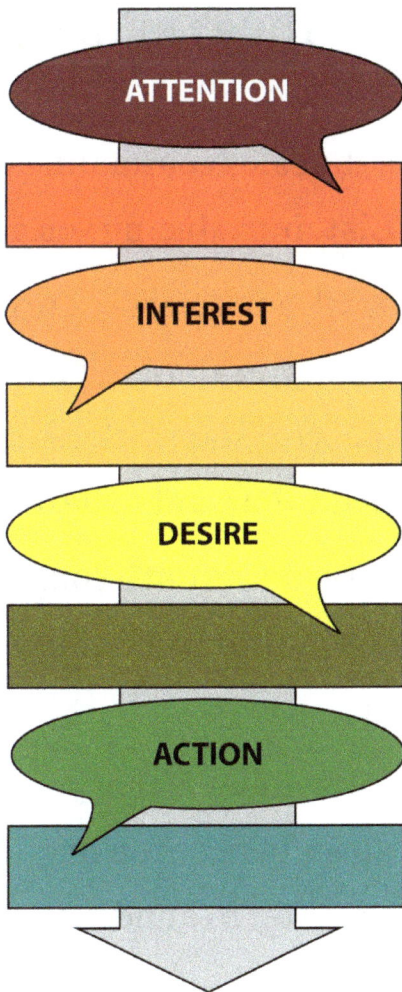

YOUR LETTER

Your **Letter** is the sales communication you send to people on your **List**, introducing you and your offer.

It can be an email, a postcard—a text message, even—but the most eye-catching medium is often a plain old envelope with stamp. Because nobody does that these days. And you want to be different, right?

If you can make sending out a couple of letters a day a habit, you will be in the top 1% of freelancers within a year. Guaranteed.

First thing to remember is that you're writing to an individual, not an audience. You may be sending a similar communication to hundreds of people, but each reads it alone. When writing, pick a person on your List and write to *him*.

Second, think benefits, not features. People don't buy drills, they buy holes. Every time you find yourself writing about what you do, turn it around and think what value it creates for your *reader*.

One acronym matters: AIDA. The paragraphs of your Letter, sentences of your postcard, or lulz of your txt-spk need to gain the reader's ==Attention, Interest, and Desire, then drive an Action.== *In that order*.

(Hipster marketer. Ignore. You know the drill.)

Of course, each Letter needs a personalised salutation—never, *ever* send a letter to a job title. Or a Whom it May Concern. Or an *info@*. But if you're clever, you'll customise a few words in your body text for each individual too, with information from your List. If you're *really* clever, you'll formalise your List annotations into standard fields so you can mailmerge them. ("Sam, I enjoy <<bollywood movies>> too.")

And if you're really, *really* clever (or have read **100 Days, 100 Grand**) you'll personalise not just snatches and snippets, but *entire phrases and paragraphs*, turning a few dozen structured sentences into a resource that makes every sales prospect feel like your only sales prospect. Meaningfully customising every marketing communication you ever send.

When you write your Letter, make it personal.

USING A SALES FUNNEL

The greatest problem in freelancing is feast-or-famine. You'll have months, even years, maxed out with a packed calendar . . . then some outside event will set off alarums and excursions, and suddenly you're up that place without a paddle. (Hi, Brexit!)

This is the (one) vulnerable aspect to being a niche player. Because you're doing that thing you like, for people you like, all your clients are likely to be in the same industry sector. So economic shocks give them all the same business problems, and they all get rid of their freelancers at the same time.

You solve this with a **sales funnel**.

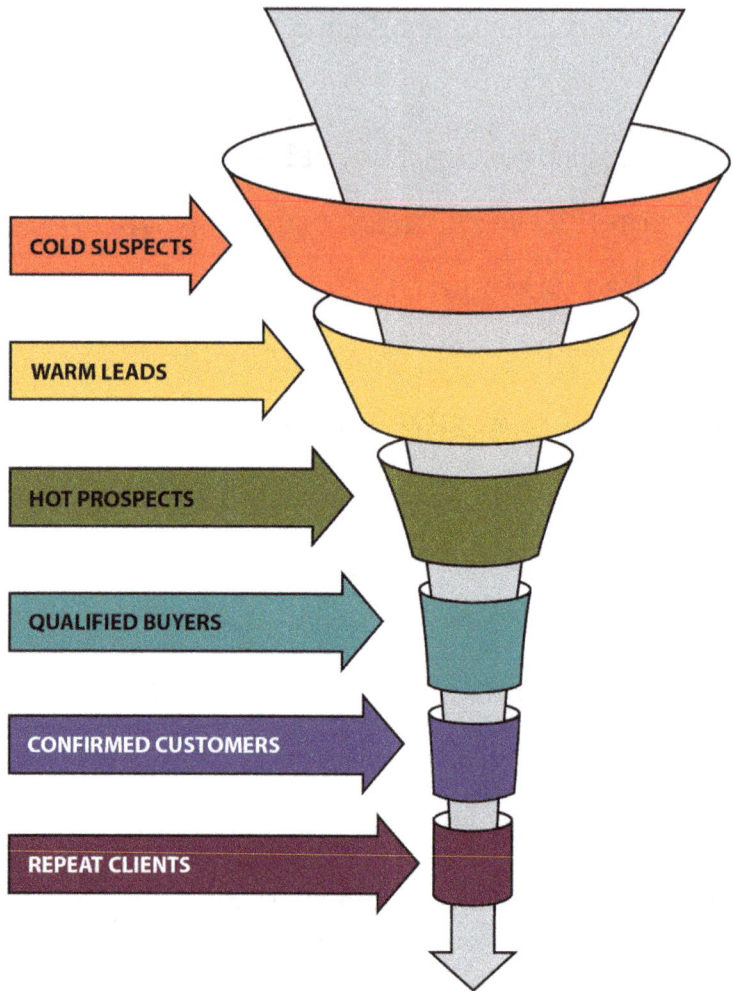

COLD SUSPECTS

WARM LEADS

HOT PROSPECTS

QUALIFIED BUYERS

CONFIRMED CUSTOMERS

REPEAT CLIENTS

A sales funnel is a simple tool for keeping your calendar solidly booked in good times *and* bad. Draw yourself a diagram, wide bit at the top.

When you add people to your List, they're *cold suspects*: people you think you could work for but who don't know you yet. One level down, where it's a bit thinner, are your *warm leads*: those who've read your **Letter**, or checked out your website.

Further down are your *hot prospects*: people you've had a chat or email with. Then come your *qualified buyers*, those actively interested in services like yours; *confirmed customers* ready to try you out with an initial project or three; and, right at the bottom in the thinnest part, *repeat clients*.

The basic thing about sales funnels: what you get out at the bottom depends on what you put in at the top.

==Marketing is a numbers game.==

If your **conversion rate** is 1%, you need to find a hundred cold suspects to get one repeat client. If you want two clients, you need to double the number of cold suspects or convert them at 2%. That's all.

The magic bit: if you make a habit of spending a couple of hours each week finding names to put into the top of your funnel, you're future-proofing your sales roster.

Let's say it takes two months to move a name from your List to that first paying project, and you know your conversion rate is 2%. If there are 50 names at the top of your funnel, you know you'll have a new customer in eight weeks. Make it 200 names, and your calendar will be packed with four of 'em.

(You don't need to *draw* the funnel, btw. Six rows on a spreadsheet can keep track of everything.)

When you get good at sales funnels, you can stir in all sorts of measures and metrics that help. Is only one in every thousand leads resulting in a hot prospect? There's something wrong with your Letter. Or are you getting plenty of initial projects, but no repeat customers? Look again at your offer.

Your **List** contains suspects. Your **Letter** turns them into prospects. Your **sales funnel** tells you whether or not they're *working*.

YOUR WEBSITE

Your website is the *least* important part of your marketing.

Sacrilege? Don't get me wrong: you've got to *have* a site. But you don't need to treat it as the be-all and end-all of customer acquisition and retention, because *your customers aren't on it*.

Today, just two websites get half of all web traffic. A handful more get most of the rest. The web today happens on phones and pads, not desktops. Nobody ever uses search on a site; nobody even types in a URL any more. Which means you don't need to spend much on your website.

(Unless, of course, your *business* is websites. *Then* you'll need a good one.)

Your website needs three pages. A **home page** illustrating your offer to the market. A page **about you**, showing visitors what makes you tick. And, of course, a **contact page**.

If you create stuff, add a (small) portfolio of your best work. (*Not* *all your work*, please.) If you do consulting stuff, add a few Case Studies. Demonstrate what value you created so visitors don't have to think.

You also need a LinkedIn profile. (A *good* one. Get professional help if needed.) And add yourself to Google My Business. If you can persuade a few people in related sectors to link to your home page, great.

Don't start a blog; it'll peter out. Don't set up a cornucopia of social media; it'll sap your energy. And *definitely* don't *buy* Likes, or Followers, or Friends, from the web's grubbier corners. It's dishonest and it doesn't work.

Much marketing bullshit is also expounded about SEO, or Search Engine Optimisation. Don't worry about this either. Just write your site text plainly and clearly with your target audience in mind, and Google will get what you're about.

Again, be yourself.

RETAINER AGREEMENTS

It is far, far easier to keep an existing customer than find a new one. Accordingly, successful freelancing is mostly about retaining the customers you already have. That's why, when you've got a repeat client on your roster, it's time to go for the Holy Grail of freelancing: the **retainer agreement**.

A retainer is a written contract with a repeat client that pays you a set fee every month for a set scope of work. As you work on a retainer contract, you'll find two things happen:

a) You get better at the work each month;
b) It takes you less time each month.

In other words, you're delivering greater value to your client, *every month*, for fewer hours down. That's what successful freelancing is all about: making the relationship ever more valuable to both sides.

So the endgame of marketing is the retainer contract. But there is one *very* important point here:

Your retainer contract needs to specify what you *won't* do as well as what you *will*.

If you don't draw this difference, you'll find your client sneaking more and work into the scope each month. Worse, you'll find yourself doing it. So make it plain from the outset what's covered in the retainer fee and what isn't. (But which you *will* do for extra cash.)

Make the retainer agreement your goal.

CLIENT RELATIONSHIPS

In today's algorithmic, programmatic, artificially intelligent world, touchy-feely human stuff like warmth and trust matter more than ever.

Why? Because they're the points of difference that decide whether a confirmed customer with an initial project turns into a repeat client who signs a retainer.

So make sure you invest time in the most important aspect of freelancing: your **client relationships**.

How? Easy. Just treat them as *people*. Learn the names of their children, what they do at weekends, their hopes and dreams for their lives. Always send greetings cards. Always say thank you when they've helped, and offer to help in return. These few little actions make a world of difference.

This is how human beings have fostered relationships for *millennia*. The only confusing thing is why so many think a business relationship can be reduced purely to money.

As an aside, this is why you should *never* use web markets like Guru, Upwork, and Fiverr (ugh). It's not about the fees they charge (high) or the rates they pay (low). It's because their business model is to *own the client relationship*.

And the client relationship belongs to *you*.

THE FREELANCE WORKPLACE

Finally, a word on the *where* of working as a successful freelancer.

Most freelancers work from home. That's fine. Work doesn't care where it gets done, and nor do most clients. (You might even rock that cliché of working in your PJs.)

But whatever your preferred approach, whether it's suited-and-booted or sofa-slacking, make sure you *know what it is* so you can do your best work. If something feels off, change your routine or rituals.

And if you work at home, don't neglect another relationship: the one with your other half. *Especially* if that other half works a "normal" job.

The basic bargain: make sure you **pay your own way**. See "Freelancing is work" above.) If your freelancing isn't paying, you're not freelancing.

The second bargain: **you do the chores**. (Be still, my heart.) You've got an extra two hours in your day, after all. Keep the floor clean, the kitchen stocked, and the table tidy. (Hey, you use it more.) And always, always meet her at the airport.

Last, understand that no matter how hard you try, nobody will *ever* truly accept you're "working". They just won't. So don't worry about it.

Remember the freelance life *is* better than most people's lives. And you're the one living it.

ABOUT CHRIS

Chris Worth is a London-based copywriter and author of the guide to effective freelancing **100 Days, 100 Grand**. Google it or head for 100days100grand.com.

At work, he creates campaigns and content backed by meaningful insights, mostly for technology clients. (He does the research and analysis too, btw—his USP.)

Interests include adventure travel and extreme sports. He's lived in six countries, visited 60, and is a qualified sky *and* scuba diver with a passion for calisthenics and kettlebells. But he's never without his Kindle. See him at chrisdoescontent.com.